Trials and Successes: Effective Teaching and Learning at Home

STEPHANIE CARTER

T0204630

© 2020 by STePH Publishing, LLC

Design and layout by Kendall King, KKPRODUCTIONS

This book has been developed for informational purposes only. The opinions, material, and conclusions are provided on the understanding that the author is not responsible for the results of any actions taken on the basis of the information provided in any article, publication, document or other form of communication to a person using said information. The statements, opinions, and conclusions offered in this book are that of the author individually and are not reflective or indicative of the opinions of any entity mentioned in this book. All information contained herein is based on the author's personal studies, research, and experience.

All rights reserved. No part of this publication may be copied, reproduced, distributed, or transmitted in any form or by any means, - electronic, mechanical, photocopy, recording, or any other – except for brief quotations in printed or online reviews, without prior written permission of the publisher. Neither the author nor the publisher assumes any responsibility for mistakes, oversights, or omissions offered in this book in respect of anything and the consequences of anything, done, or omitted to be done by any such person in reliance, whether wholly or partially, upon the whole or any part of the contents of this book. Furthermore, no liability is assumed for any damages or outcomes resulting from the use of information composed herein.

This book identifies product names and services known to be trademarks, registered trademarks, or service marks of their respective holders. They are used throughout this book in an editorial fashion only. STePH Publishing, LLC is not associated with any company or product mentioned in this book.

TRIALS AND SUCCESSES: EFFECTIVE TEACHING AND LEARNING AT HOME/STEPHANIE CARTER – 1st Edition

ISBN: 978-1-7353141-0-5

First Printing, July 2020

Printed in the United States of America

For more information, visit http://www.stephaniecarter.net

Dedication

I dedicate this book to all of the parents and guardians who step out on faith to take on the tremendous responsibility and task of educating their children.

Acknowledgments

I would like thank my Heavenly Father God—Thank you for your Son, my Savior and Lord, for blessing me with a wonderful husband and sons, and for blessing me with the opportunity to homeschool.

To my dear husband, Phillip Carter—Thank you for your love and unwavering support and for encouraging me to write this book. I love and appreciate you so much.

To my sons, Stephen and Thomas—Thank you for being wonderful sons and students. I thank God every day for giving me the tremendous honor of being not only your teacher but your mom. I look forward to the amazing things He has in store for you both.

To my parents, Henry and Carolyn Knox, my siblings, my extended family, and friends—Thank you for supporting and loving me throughout the years.

To Anita Williams—Thank you for all of your help in the editing and preparation of the book. The laughs kept me going.

To Wendy McLean—Thank you for your consultation and advice. You are an inspiration to many homeschool parents.

To Tammy Padilla—Thank you for pushing me to the finish line.

To Kendall King—Thank you for using your God-given talent to design the cover and guide me through this process.

Table of Contents

Introduction

With the pandemic of 2020, many parents have been forced to do something similar to what I've been doing for the last 11 years, teach your children at home and/or participate in some form of online learning. Homeschooling is a huge, sometimes difficult adjustment for you and your children. In this book, I will discuss my journey, and provide information, guidance and encouragement to those who wish to take charge of their child's education and start the process of homeschooling. It will take courage and a willingness to learn and implement the ideas described throughout this book.

"Character cannot be developed in ease and quiet. Only through experience of trial and suffering can the soul be strengthened, ambition inspired, and success achieved."

Helen Keller

This book is not for those that believe that formal education is the only standard. If you feel that way, stop reading now. This book is for those who are willing to travel the road less traveled and are willing to try an out-of-the-box approach to their child's education.

I'm your tour guide. This book is to guide you, but not dictate to you, because every child, every household, every situation is different. This book contains lessons and ideas that have worked in *my* household and with *my* sons during years and years of trials and successes. Apply what you think can work. Skip what you think can't work. Let's go.

Chapter 1
SO YOU WANT TO HOMESCHOOL?

There are several terms for what people today call, "homeschooling." Some call it home education. Others call it home teaching. Another popular term is home learning. These are all fine and I will use these terms interchangeably throughout. Whether you prefer the term homeschooling, home education, home teaching, home learning, my personal definition of the term is education that

> *"Whenever you find yourself on the side of the majority, it is time to pause and reflect."*
> *Mark Twain*

takes place outside of a traditional school for which a parent or guardian takes full responsibility and, therefore, determines what the child learns, how the child learns, where the child learns, and who teaches the child.

When you home educate, your child's education—from what is taught to how it's taught—is in your hands. While some define homeschooling as your child receiving assignments from a traditional school teacher, to be completed at home, this is actually distance learning, which occurs when your child is physically apart from their teacher. This is what a lot of children are doing during the COVID 19 pandemic. Distance learning is often mislabeled as homeschooling because it involves doing school work at home; however, it is not homeschooling.

When you homeschool, your child's education is in your hands. It is educational freedom. But like most freedoms, not everyone can handle it. You have to have discipline. You have to be responsible. You have to be honest with yourself that you *can* do it. Most importantly, you have to be trusted that you *will* do it. Taking charge of anything is no easy task and taking charge of your child's education is one of the hardest and most challenging tasks that you will face, but, take it from someone who has been on this journey for 11 years, the reward is and will be worth it all. If you are willing and able and if it is the best option for you, your child, and your household, you can home teach your child for as long as you want.

Also, like most freedoms, there are many people who feel that you should not be afforded this freedom because it should be reserved for others. In this instance, the freedom to educate your child should be reserved for anyone who has acquired an education degree or anyone with experience in the field of education. An overwhelming majority of people feel this way, and that's fine. I understand why they believe that. Everybody sends their child to school. The educational responsibility is the school system's. Not to mention, you get the freedom of having your child under another institution's care for six to eight hours a day for five days a week for nine months a year. So I understand why people would question why homeschooling families would give up the freedom of less educational responsibility to have the freedom of complete educational responsibility. But each family has their reasons, and throughout the book, you will learn mine.

Also, with this freedom, there are many sacrifices. One sacrifice is financial. Many home teaching families choose to forgo two full time incomes for one. Decisions are made to cut costs and/or reassign them.. Reassigned because later you will discover that homeschooling your child is not cheap and wise financial decisions will carry you along the way. Another sacrifice is mental. You will receive scrutiny and feel the need to justify your reason to homeschool. As I mentioned earlier, as a home educator, you are a minority, and the minority are always scrutinized. People will ask questions. Some questions will be genuine. People will also ask your child questions, either to be curious or to test your child. You will learn about my experience with this in the next chapter. You'll have to stay strong in the face of this scrutiny and remind yourself that *your* reason(s) for home teaching *your* child is all the justification you need.

That freedom and right to educate your child is reserved for whoever is willing to have it and is worth the sacrifices that come with it. I believed it was the best decision when my husband and I decided to home teach 11 years ago, and it is the best decision for me to continue until I can hand them their walking papers on Graduation Day.

NOTES/THINGS TO REMEMBER

_____

_____

_____

_____

_____

_____

_____

_____

_____

_____

_____

_____

Chapter 2
MY START

My life definitely changed in order for me to write this book. It changed from being a plane-hopping, career-oriented woman to the homeschooling, stay-at-home mom I am today. Let me explain. When I graduated from college, I set career goals, which I was determined to meet. One goal was to become a Certified Public Accountant (CPA), which I did in 1999. Another was to become a partner of a public accounting firm. I wanted to travel around the world. However, in the back of my mind, I wanted to get married. I wanted to have a family. Until then, I was focused on my career. I was working 16+ hour days. I was flying everywhere. I was climbing up my career ladder. April of 1999 changed all of that.

During April 1999, each week a person that I knew died. During the first week, a hit-and-run driver killed one of my cousins. A week later, on the day of my cousin's funeral, I found out that the son of my aunt's neighbor, with whom I grew up, was killed in a motorcycle accident. Seven days later, my father's best friend died after a long illness. Finally, my favorite preacher of my church's annual revival died of cancer.

These deaths had a huge impact on how I was spending my life. I was spending the majority of my young life pursuing my career, but I had no time for myself. So, the next month, May 1999, I shifted.

In May 1999, I decided to look for a job where I could work only eight hours a day and a job that allowed me to arrive at the same time and leave at the same time every day.

I was blessed with that kind of job and I had more time for myself. I joined a bowling league. I spent more time with friends. Then, I began dating Phillip Carter and a year and a half later, we married. Four years later, we had our first son, Stephen. I wanted to be a full-time, stay-at-home mom. I didn't want to go back to work. My job denied my request to telecommute. Although they allowed me to work from home for 3 months after Stephen was born, I was miserable. Two years later, we had our second son, Thomas. After Thomas was born, the idea of going back to work was unbearable. I don't know if I was dealing with postpartum depression, but the thought of going back to work and leaving my boys in daycare put me in a very dark place.

I would mention in conversations about staying home but I don't think anyone ever knew the extent to which I was struggling.

One day, I was rocking Thomas to sleep in his nursery when Phil walked in. He sat on a chair, facing me and asked, "Do you want to stay home?" I was in shock. Did he just ask me if I wanted to stay home? I nodded. He said that he felt that I needed to be home. He said okay and just like that, the conversation was finished, just like his marriage proposal (I will explain in the next book). I sent in my notice, and I was officially a stay-at-home mom. I guess you could say that was the day when the initial seed of homeschooling was planted,  although we didn't know it yet, but Phil paved the way to it.

I don't remember the first time I heard about homeschooling. There were two things I knew for sure. The first thing was that no teacher, whether in public school or private school, would ever know my child as well as I, nor invest in their education the way I could. The second thing I knew was that my boys understood things more like their father and that their attention spans weren't ideal for the traditional school setting.

I bet you're saying that most boys are like that. Yes, I know, but as the mother to two African-American boys in America, I felt an urge, for their future, to do something different because African-American boys and men are treated differently.

When my oldest son was four years old, I began to research homeschooling, even though I had already begun teaching him. I had read stories to him since he was a baby. I was already teaching him his ABC's and 123's. I approached my husband about homeschooling. To be honest, I was concerned about his reaction since he was and still is an educator. We discussed the pros and cons, and after much discussion and research, we decided to home teach.

When we told family and friends about our decision, the response was as expected: some positive, some negative. As I mentioned earlier, when you are in the minority, you will be scrutinized. Anytime you do the opposite of the status quo, you should expect mixed reactions and a lot of questions. We were asked the typical questions asked of most homeschooling parents: the "socialization" question, the "same level as their peers" question, the "normal" questions. You may have asked one of these questions yourself.

As our sons grew, a few friends and family tested them by asking them math questions or asking them to read something. It was subtle, but I knew what they were doing and why.

It was because of the assumption that since my sons were homeschooled, either they weren't learning anything or they weren't learning as much as kids their age in traditional school. Again, I was unqualified to teach them because I wasn't an education major so, of course, they couldn't be learning anything, right? Stephen is at high school level and Thomas is close to it. That speaks for itself.

Although these encounters made me angry, they did some good. It created a chip on my shoulder, and that chip has given me the drive to graduate my sons. Believe it or not, as they have gotten older, the teaching has become more fun. We are having intriguing conversations as we learn and discover together. I've seen them mature as they've seen me age.

For me, homeschooling is a calling because I felt the urge to educate my sons, and now, I can't imagine doing anything else. Every day, I wake up excited about what we'll learned that day. This homeschooling journey has not been perfect. There's been ups and downs, elation and tears, but overall, the journey has been awesome.

NOTES/THINGS TO REMEMBER

_____

_____

_____

_____

_____

_____

_____

_____

_____

_____

_____

_____

_____

_____

Chapter 3
YOUR ROLE AS A HOME EDUCATOR

I mentioned earlier that as a home educator, you take complete responsibility for your child's education into your own hands. In doing so, you will wear many hats. Along with your home and/or work responsibilities, you will be the teacher, the administrator, the principal, the dean of students, the guidance counselor, the lunch lady/man, and the bus driver. But these roles can be consolidated into roles of a teacher and, more importantly, a guide.

I like to use the analogy of a museum tour guide to describe my role as a home educator. My sons and I have visited a lot of museums over the years so I love this analogy. A museum's tour guide directs us along and shows us everything that there is to see. They describe the interesting, the good, the bad, the boring, all of it. They may tell you about the exhibit and maybe a personal experience, but they leave you to your own interpretation of the exhibit. They don't tell you how an exhibit is supposed to make you feel. Most of the time, the tour guide will ask you about your feelings. They may influence you to take another point of view, but they don't dictate your comprehension of it.

As a home educator, my purpose is to inform and give my child the opportunity to interpret what they are discovering and to watch their world open and come alive. Now, the tour guide may warn us not to touch the exhibits. Just the same, we, as home teachers, are to discipline our children and teach them right from wrong, and let them know what is good and what is not.

Also, you are to guide your child on a path that is specifically designed for them to fulfill their purpose. This is one of the clear advantages of home education—you can mold your child's education to fit his or her unique gifts and challenges. I apply that unique purpose principle to education— to guide your child

to that place, career, business, and purpose for their life. Home education gives you the flexibility to discover the uniqueness of your child and customize your child's education to their unique gifts and abilities.

So during my many years of homeschooling, I've learned to guide my sons' education and their learning through different experiences, methods, trials, and successes.

Home educators are available for different times and different seasons of your child's life. For some, like me, you homeschooled from the beginning and plan to graduate your child. There are others who homeschool until high school, and others who homeschool for a year. Whatever the case, when you decided to homeschool, you decided to take your child's education into your hands. That's why you have to know that you want to do this because it will seem overwhelming. That's why I believe it is a calling and you should have the urging to home teach. It takes determination and discipline and you have to give it your all.

NOTES/THINGS TO REMEMBER

Chapter 4

UNDERSTAND HOMESCHOOLING

As of this printing, approximately 2.3 million kids ages 5 to 17 are homeschooled in the United States. There are a variety of reasons why. Some families want to educate their children based on their religious beliefs. Some families teach at home because of the quality of the local public school system. Others do it because they need a more flexible lifestyle because of frequent moves, i.e., a military family, or because of a child prodigy whose family wishes to dedicate more time to honing that gift. Other reasons include bullying concerns, special needs attention, or kids who struggle in traditional school settings. There are so many reasons. The common thread is the opportunity to define the type of education you wish your child to receive.

I mentioned earlier our main reason to homeschool, but there were others. My husband and I wanted to center our sons' education on an Afro-centric perspective, with Biblical principles, and an entrepreneurial mindset. We didn't want our sons to have the typical Euro-centric based curriculum that is taught in traditional schools.

We wanted to emphasize African history, its people, and its culture. Furthermore, we wanted our sons to understand the rich history of African-Americans in this country including the sacrifices, the struggles, and the accomplishments in making what the United States is today. I was very firm on that issue. I went to a private school, and the only black history I was taught was that African-Americans were slaves and the slaves were freed. I learned about the Civil Rights Movement because I chose the subject for my senior research paper, not because it was taught in my history class. I still remember a lot of my research because I actively pursued the information. This is an aspect of homeschooling that I'll discuss later.

Sidebar: Did you know that people still call Africa a country, not a continent with 54 countries? It's amazing how many people still believe this. Some of this is because of the traditional curriculum.

Regarding the entrepreneurial aspect, we want our children to understand that the goal for getting a great education is not just to obtain a job—that can be one path but not the only path. As adults, they can choose to become entrepreneurs and own their own businesses, thus being self employed.

When deciding to homeschool, weigh the advantages and disadvantages based on your family dynamic. Homeschooling may not be conducive to your lifestyle; every family is different. Home education requires major sacrifice, which can be overwhelming, and a certain amount of flexibility that is not always conducive to a family that requires structure. Factors such as time restraints, stringent commitments and responsibilities, such as the care of a loved one, may factor into your decision to home school.

NOTES/THINGS TO REMEMBER

Chapter 5
QUESTIONS ANSWERED

When you decide to home teach, it can be freeing to some while terrifying to others. There will be moments of anxiousness and self-doubt. All of these emotions are okay, and there are some common questions that new homeschooling parents and those who are contemplating homeschooling tend to ask.

Am I Qualified to Home Teach? My answer is always, "Absolutely!!" You may not know it. You may not believe it. You are. You know your child better than anyone else—at least, you should. You were your child's first teacher. You are your child's best teacher. You've been teaching them from birth. Just because they become school aged doesn't mean that your teaching should end.
Yes, there will be those who think that you're not qualified, but

don't believe that. More importantly, your child can learn. They will learn if your teaching is consistent and regular. Your child has been learning since the day they were born. They learned to walk, to eat with a spoon and fork, to drink from a cup, to talk. You can teach and your child can learn.

Can I Do It? The answer: Yes, you can. It won't be easy, and let me emphasize this by underlining, bolding, italicizing, and capitalizing that point: ***<u>IT WON'T BE EASY</u>***. It will require all of the things that one has when learning something new: effort, consistency, discipline, determination, patience, and perseverance.

What If I Don't Know Everything? You won't know everything. You don't need to know everything, either. You can learn at the same time you can teach. In fact, it is always fun when you and your child learn together. You will discover that your child will be more engaged because you will be engaged. This will result in more interaction and discussion between you and your child and, even better, a closer connection. I believe this is the reason why many home teaching parents become Jeopardy contestants and champions. Home teachers learn as they teach.

What If I Don't Have The Patience?

I hear this a lot, "I don't have the patience to teach my kids." I don't know of any home teaching parent who has all of the patience needed. I call it the "patience tank;" it doesn't come "full." Your patience tank has to be consistently filled because it is used as soon as it is  full. When your patience tank is almost empty, take some time for yourself and recharge. Use your tag team partner (see chapter 9). Remember, home teaching is like cultivating fertile soil—it is a process. It takes work, persistence, and patience.

NOTES/THINGS TO REMEMBER

Chapter 6

WHAT SHOULD YOU DO?

As home educators or if you are thinking of starting this journey with your child, there are some things that you should do and know.

Know and Understand Your Jurisdiction's Homeschool Laws and Guidelines.
When contemplating home education, there are laws and guidelines that differ from state to state and county to county. Homeschooling is legal in all 50 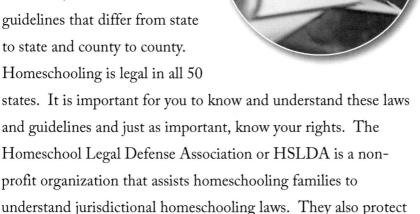 states. It is important for you to know and understand these laws and guidelines and just as important, know your rights. The Homeschool Legal Defense Association or HSLDA is a non-profit organization that assists homeschooling families to understand jurisdictional homeschooling laws. They also protect the freedom to homeschool and will provide legal representation when necessary.

You can make your decision to homeschool at any time during the year. You can decide to start when your child is four/five or when your child is 15 and attending a traditional school. You should consult with your state and local laws to determine whether you need to notify your local board of education and whether or not you're required to file paperwork in order to homeschool your child legally. Some states are stricter than others. Some states require a homeschooling parent or guardian to have a high school diploma, others don't. Know what to do so that your freedom to homeschool is protected.

Teach Consistently and Regularly. Did you notice that I said teach regularly? It does not read, "teach daily." Home teachers need breaks, too. Don't think that you need to teach every day for your child to "keep up" or "get ahead" (learn more about that later). Be consistent. Be dedicated. Teach regularly. Because remember, your child will learn daily.

Keep a Portfolio/Record of Your Teaching and Their Learning. You should also keep lasting memories of your consistent and regular teaching. Take pictures of your child's activities and projects. Make copies of the certificates when your child completes a level. Keep the certificates of achievement when they complete that co-op course. Doing this will document the progress made and it will document the days that will soon be gone. Doing this will also help you generate a portfolio if it's required by your state.

Homeschool portfolios provide evidence of what your child has learned, materials used, and their progress. Your portfolio may include but is not limited to syllabi, lists of materials used (text and resource books, online learning transcripts, computer programs), assignment samples from each subject, reading logs, participation and awards certificates, field trip pictures, writing samples, and anything that will best represent your homeschool activities.

As each homeschool is unique, so are portfolios. For example, the content of your portfolio will depend on your method of teaching. Unschooling families will not have a list of textbooks while school-at-home families would. I will discuss homeschool teaching methods later in the book. You can also customize the way your portfolio is presented. Nowadays, families keep their portfolio content electronically with scanned documents and uploaded pictures. Other homeschool families organize hard paper copies in accordion folders, color-coded files, or three-ring binders. You decide what is best for you.

Depending on your jurisdiction, you may be required to have a portfolio review, usually on a quarterly or annual basis. If your jurisdiction requires a portfolio review, you may choose to either present your portfolio to a homeschooling representative of the local county or you can enroll in an umbrella program. An umbrella program is an oversight program, usually provided by a homeschool co-op or religious organization that oversees your homeschool to ensure that it fulfills all state requirements.

I believe portfolios should be compiled for every child for every year as a record of accomplishment and progress over the years regardless of whether it's required or not. When I look at my son's work and pictures of their projects and our field trips at seven years ago or three years ago, I'm amazed at the progress.

Plant the Right Seeds. If you didn't know by now, I love analogies. Earlier I spoke about home teaching parents sowing into fertile ground. What seeds are you planting? The seeds you plant are the plants you'll produce. If you plant strawberry seeds, you'll expect to receive strawberries. If you plant corn seeds, you should receive corn. If you plant poison, you will get poison. We need to remember that when we home teach our children, we are the farmers. Our children's lives are fertile ground and we're planting seeds into their education every day. We're planting seeds of arithmetic, reading, writing, wisdom, critical thinking skills, good study habits, responsibility, good stewardship, good conversational skills to name a few. As always, since home teaching is customized and personalized, the seeds that are planted differ from home to home. In my household, in addition to the seeds listed above, we also plant seeds of entrepreneurship, seeds of investing skills, seeds of serving others, and seeds of discovering different

cultures through our international travels. What seeds do you currently plant or will you plant with your home education? Write them down and use them as goals for achievement for your child and for you.

Expect Some Scrutiny and Pushback. Although there are more than two million homeschoolers in this country, homeschooling isn't common or popular. Many people still think that homeschooling is inadequate, fake education. Some even call it a fringe movement. You will receive scrutiny and even question the quality of your home education, especially if your inner circle includes professionally-trained educators. Do expect people to offer their "advice" about your decision to be responsible for your child's education, even when you didn't ask for their advice. Be confident in knowing that the decision that you made is the decision that is best for your child and your family. Don't let anyone make you feel less of a parent or less of a person because you homeschool. Remember the reason you made the decision, remember your vision, and remember your goal.

Go With the Flow and Have Fun. I want to take this time to encourage you now and not at the end of the book. Whether you're just starting to home teach or you've been on this journey for a while, it is important to go with the flow while you are still "steering the ship." Also, have fun with this experience because it will be over before you know it. It will be overwhelming but count it all joy. If a curriculum or program works, stick with it. If it doesn't, try something new. Your child will learn. You may have to take it slow or even slower. Wait for the AHA! moment.

This journey is a marathon, not a sprint. Homeschooling will be hard for you and your child. It is a labor of love. I've cried. I've fallen on my knees. I've also experienced the joy in my sons' faces in the "AHA!" moments after days, if not weeks, in the darkness of "I don't know," or "I don't understand," or "Why do I need to know this?" I believe that home teaching is a rewarding experience with a lot of trial and error. Keep in mind to go with the flow and have fun. Enjoy the "I don't knows" as well as the "AHAs."

NOTES/THINGS TO REMEMBER

Chapter 7

WHAT YOU SHOULDN'T DO?

I mentioned that I don't want to dictate, but there are things that I suggest you not do in order to either keep your sanity or to keep moving forward.

> *"Experience is learning a lot of things you shouldn't do..."*
> William S. Knudsen

Don't Pressure. Sometimes, we put too much pressure on our children to succeed, and we feel that if they don't know the material or understand it when it is presented, then something is wrong. I've discovered that each child will learn in their own time and they will discover that they like it in their own time, not someone else's. This is further from the truth and as we continue along this journey, I am opening up to more revelations about my children and just how special they are. I also realize that just because your child is not gifted in math does not mean your child is any less smart than those who are. Why it is that math is used as the benchmark for how smart a person is? We need to stop that.

Of course, we need math and we need to read in order to function in this world.

Don't Be Pressured—Often. Not succumbing to pressure is easier said than done. You will feel the pressure when your child is not on the same level as your child's peers, according to perceived "standards." When my sons were being "tested" by my friends and family, they were usually asked a math question. Why? Because traditionally, children are measured by how well they read, write, and calculate math. If your child is not great in a "core" subject, homeschooling gives you the flexibility to allow your child to learn at their own pace and concentrate on specific areas. Be patient. Use *your* judgment and seek help if you find it to be necessary. You must learn or change your mindset of not fitting your child in a box. You may feel bad when they might not be able to do what others can at a certain age. You can either give in to the peer pressure or you keep your eyes on the prize.

Realize that your child's gifts and abilities may be in an area that is not measured by a math or reading question. It is important for us to guide our children and to apply their knowledge to be successful in the world we live. My sons haven't attended a traditional school. They know how to read. They know how to write. They know how to research. It took time. More importantly, they can demonstrate their critical thinking skills to apply what they've learned over the years to their everyday lives. As parents and homeschoolers, that should be our end goal.

Don't Compare. One thing that home teachers love to do is compare. We compare kids, curricula, recipes, co-ops, grades, teaching styles, you name it. It is okay to talk and bounce off ideas, but just remember that each home is different. Just because it works for one household doesn't mean that it will work for yours. So listen to the advice and research the ideas that you've heard or read and be the judge and jury for your home school. If you decide to try an idea, program, or curriculum and if it works, that's great! If it doesn't, leave it be and move on. Don't force it. It doesn't mean that you're a failure. Believe me, it can make you feel that way. I've spent hundreds of dollars on curricula that I was advised was the greatest curricula on earth and it turned out to be a disaster. I bet it was a great program, but not for my sons. The greatest curricula on earth turned into a great sale for my eBay account.

Don't Believe Homeschooling Is Cheap. Homeschooling can get expensive because homeschool parents must cover all of the homeschooling costs and they can really add up. If you buy curricula and supplies for each subject for each child, that can get rather expensive. Co-ops may charge per class, per child. Nation-wide homeschool programs like Classical Conversations can be very expensive. Food is an expense to think about since you're home most days. Then there are costs for field trips, online classes, and dual enrollment, when your child is enrolled in a college when in high school. If you are switching from a traditional school where these costs are covered, you might be in for a shock when these costs add up.

So homeschooling can be expensive, but it doesn't have to be. You costs can be determined by who you homeschool and how you homeschool. Of course, the costs increases with the number of children, and the School-At-Home method will be more expensive than unschooling or eclectic method. But there are plenty of ways to mitigate the costs by swapping books and supplies with another homeschool family, buying on eBay, using your local library, taking advantage of free programs, and more.

Budgeting is the key. The majority of homeschooling families are one-income households, although many homeschooling parents have at-home businesses to supplement income. So homeschooling is a financial sacrifice, but families find the sacrifice well worth it because their kids reap the invaluable benefits of being home schooled.

Don't Believe Homeschooling Is Easy. You're going to have hard days as a home teacher. PERIOD. It can be stressful for the parent and for the child. There will be days when your child doesn't want to do the work or be obedient. There's a lot more distractions at home that you will need to manage. It takes a lot of trial, error, and success to determine which teaching method and type of homeschool will best fit your child at each age and at each phase of the learning process. You will have days when you will need to encourage yourself. Remind yourself of the reason(s) you decided to homeschool and your goals you wish to accomplish. In doing so, you'll find the tenacity and confidence in what you're doing. It might not happen quickly, but continue to move forward. Don't stop. These hard days will make your reward that much more valuable. That is the blessed hope.

Don't Stop the Questions. One of the advantages of homeschooling is the time it allows for your child to ask questions. Children are naturally curious. They ask questions, lots of questions. This should be encouraged. Why? For one, it creates dialogue, which is communication. Children who are used to asking questions will naturally seek out answers to their questions on their own as they age. As your child gets older, they may become more curious about the things that you do. The questions may be tough and serious, but they should not be ignored and should trigger conversation and beneficial dialogue.

TRIALS AND SUCCESSES: EFFECTIVE TEACHING AND LEARNING AT HOME

NOTES/THINGS TO REMEMBER

_____

_____

_____

_____

_____

_____

_____

_____

_____

_____

_____

_____

_____

_____

_____

TRIALS AND SUCCESSES: EFFECTIVE TEACHING AND LEARNING AT HOME

Chapter 8

THE TRUTH

Just like anything else that occurs outside of the norm, there are many misconceptions about home education. I will attempt to give a little clarity to some of these misconceptions.

I Have to Teach Everything. In the first few chapters, I let you know that as a homeschooling parent or guardian, you are to guide your child's education. You can serve your role as your child's education administrator to direct how and where your child is taught. However, that doesn't mean that you have to be your child's only teacher. Many homeschool parents attend homeschool cooperative classes or co-ops where homeschoolers attend weekly classes taught by parents and/or teachers who specialize in a particular field of study. Co-ops also offer field trips or programs. You can also use online classes, videos, tutors, and community college courses to delegate your teaching duties.

> *"The trouble with the world is not that people know too little; it's that they know so many things that just aren't so."*
>
> *Mark Twain*

I love teaching my sons one-on-one, but I don't want to teach Stephen Japanese or teach Thomas mechanical engineering. I use a combination of online classes, co-op classes, and relatives who are gifted in a discipline. For example, my husband's cousin is an artist and teaches my sons Art History. You don't have to do it all.

Home Teaching Means Less Learning. Your child will learn and learn a lot. The pace of your child's learning will, of course, depend on your child. It is not about whether your child will learn or not. Believe it or not, they will and they will learn more. From the time they're born, children are naturally curious and that curiosity could be the basis of their home education. There is a familiar saying in the home teaching community that learning is better and easier when it's caught, not taught. In other words, children learn and retain information when it is discovered on their own or when they don't know they're learning. Many home teaching methods apply this approach.

Let's Talk Babies. Babies aren't taught to cry. They don't learn to cry. It is an innate behavior, meaning they are born with that skill. However, babies learn that if they cry, someone is going to pick them up or feed them.

That is not something you taught them. They learned this through consistency and repetition. They cried once. There was a response. They cried again. There was another response. Soon, they realize that if I do this, then the adult will respond. They also realize the power that they have over the adults in their life. This is the beginning of your child's road to lifelong learning. Then there's walking. Children learn to walk through trial and error. They try to stand. They fall. They try to stand again. They fall again. But with every fall, your child will rise. They will continue this process until they start walking—the method of trial and success. Did the desire to walk begin with you saying "It's time to walk?" No. It began with their desire to learn to walk. When we saw this desire, we guided and protected them. We could say the same about talking and other skills. Lessons that are taught at home have more of a lasting effect on children.

Neither one of my sons were early readers. In a traditional setting, they would have been considered late readers and may have been evaluated for special needs services. But in my homeschool, I was patient. I kept reading to them. I displayed the word and pronounced it. Of course, I would get frustrated, but I stayed consistent. They will read and they will read in their time. I planted the seeds. Then, one day, I realized that Stephen was reading the comments under the YouTube videos I assigned him (he's a visual learner). That was it. It was the curiosity or the motivation of him knowing what was said about the video. He still reads the comments and is an avid reader. He learned in his time. Thomas took even longer and he still doesn't like to read, but he has progressed year after year, and that is the key. When you see the progression, keep encouraging, keep cultivating, stay consistent. You know then that you can make it to the learning goal.

Homeschooling Is Traditional School at Home. This is not the case. I want to reiterate that if you are exclusively receiving assignments from a traditional school, and you have no control over what is being taught, you are not homeschooling. However, you can make your homeschool like a traditional school with a rigid schedule including textbooks, assignments, quizzes, and tests. This method is called the School At Home. This is not the only method, and it's not the usual method. Homeschool methods range from more traditional-like School At Home to Unschooling, which is complete student-led learning. Home Teaching allows you to choose the method that works best for you, your child, and your household. I describe the different methods of home teaching in Chapter 10.

My Child Can't Participate in Sports. There are a number of ways that homeschooled students can participate in sports, both competitively and non-competitively. Some public school systems allow homeschooled students to play competitive sports in their districts.

Check with your local school board or the HSLDA to see if this option is available to you. You may contact the private schools in your area to inquire if they allow homeschooled students to participate in their sport programs. Homeschool co-ops may also offer homeschool leagues for various sports. You can also research your local parks and recreation centers, community centers, Boys and Girls Clubs, and community colleges for classes, activities, and leagues to find the right sport for your child. In fact, many community centers and colleges are now offering sports classes specifically for homeschoolers during the day. You can also consider private lessons if you can afford it. Homeschoolers use these classes and activities to fulfill physical education requirements and help your child make new friends and acquaintances.

Homeschooling also allows you the flexibility not only in your studies but in your extracurricular activities. I invite you to think outside of the box and look at other types of sports in addition to the traditional team sports like baseball, basketball, football, soccer, etc. Individualized sports such as swimming, golf, bowling, tennis, and martial arts offer great opportunities for participation as well as scholarship opportunities in the future. In addition to baseball and basketball, my sons have participated and competed in taekwondo, bowling, golf, and fencing.

Homeschooling Means Isolation.

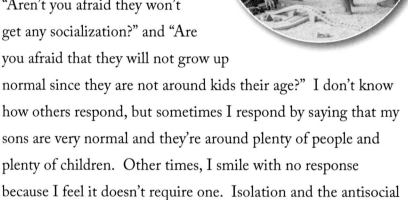

I have had to deal with the age-old questions that I bet every home educator has dealt with at some time during their home teaching journey: "Aren't you afraid they won't get any socialization?" and "Are you afraid that they will not grow up normal since they are not around kids their age?" I don't know how others respond, but sometimes I respond by saying that my sons are very normal and they're around plenty of people and plenty of children. Other times, I smile with no response because I feel it doesn't require one. Isolation and the antisocial stigma of homeschoolers is one of the biggest misconceptions.

Homeschooled children attend co-ops, homeschool days, church services, and participate in many extracurricular activities because the flexibility of the schedule allows for these activities. Some home taught children are isolated but it is the choice of that family.

You Can Only Teach at Home. A lot of home learning is accomplished with trips to museums, tours, co-ops, walks, and extracurricular activities. When my sons were younger, we went on a lot of tours. I either called the manager or supervisor of the place I wanted to visit or I set up a tour using a touring website. We toured the local Giant Food store and the local sheriff's office, just to name a few. These trips leave a lasting impression on your child and they remember what they've learned for years to come. It will teach your child to become more observant of the world around them as well as being observant of people. These activities also help them socialize because they interact with people of *all* ages by asking questions and engaging in conversation.

I Can't Homeschool My Special Needs Child. There is a wide spectrum of special needs. I have a high functioning autistic child, and it requires a little more attention on my part and his part. I also know a lot of homeschooling families with children with a range of special needs from Down's syndrome to dyslexia, and they are doing a masterful job. Just like you don't need an education degree to homeschool, you don't need a special education degree to teach your special needs child. Again, you know your child and their needs better than anybody, and your child's needs are what are most important.

Homeschooling gives parents have the unique opportunity to be more flexible and customize the curriculum to the needs of their special needs child or children who learn differently.

If you have a child with special needs, you can have your child evaluated by your local school district since federal law requires local school districts to agree to an evaluation if there's a reason to suspect that a child has a disability. This mandate, called Child Find, covers children from birth through 21 years old, including homeschoolers, and is part of the 2004 Individuals with Disabilities Education Act (IDEA). With an evaluation, your child may be eligible to receive special education services.

The type of special education services and the requirements to receive those services depend on the state or local school district.

Some states do provide eligible homeschooled children access to special education or related services, such as speech therapy. However, other states do not provide any special education services to homeschoolers and require children to attend a local public school to receive those services. Other states use a service plan that allows you to homeschool and have your child go to a local public school to receive special education services a few times per week.

In the traditional school system, an Individualized Education Plan (IEP) is a customized plan designed to meet a child's learning needs and can be developed for the purpose of receiving special education. For homeschoolers, this document is called a Student Educational Plan (SEP) or an Individualized Student Plan (ISP). If you have any questions, you may search for special education homeschool consultants, contact an HSLDA Special Needs Consultant, or contact the homeschool representative of your local public school system.

It's Hard for Homeschoolers to Get into College. Unlike popular opinion that homeschoolers are ill-prepared for college, homeschoolers are better prepared for college, outperform on pre-college exams, and are frequently recruited for colleges. A 2016 study by the National Home Education Research Institute (NHERI) indicates that home educated children scored between

15 and 30 percentage points higher on standardized academic achievement tests than those in traditional schools. A main reason for this is because test preparation is included in the curriculum of many homeschoolers.

Many colleges now have admission processes specifically for homeschooled applicants. These colleges realize that they can't use statistics such as class rank but they recognize the uniqueness of the education and rely heavily on SAT/ACT/CLT scores, academics, volunteering and extracurricular activities.

Another reason why homeschoolers are better prepared for college is because of dual enrollment. Dual enrollment occurs when your homeschooler enrolls in online college courses or courses at another educational institution like a community college in addition to their work at home. This usually occurs in 11th or 12th grade, although under certain circumstances, you can begin even earlier. Dual enrollment helps your child adjust to college-level work as well as obtain college credit. The flexibility in homeschool schedules allow for homeschoolers to do this.

College preparatory is the key to all of this, and you shouldn't wait until ninth grade to start the process. In fact, it's great if you start in middle school if that is the path you're pursuing. One program I recommend is College Prep Genius. It is a program that provides parents and students, particularly homeschoolers, with college search tips, standardized test-taking strategies, step-by-step instructions, and scholarship advice.

So just know that if you plan and prepare accordingly, your homeschooler can attend college and be successful.

NOTES/THINGS TO REMEMBER

_____

_____

_____

_____

_____

_____

_____

_____

_____

_____

_____

_____

_____

_____

Chapter 9

LESSONS LEARNED

I titled this book, *Trials and Successes*, because it summarizes everything about our homeschool journey. The above quote is a true detailed summary of it. I bet a lot of homeschooling parents and guardians can apply the quote to not only the whole journey, but to each school year. I want to offer a few lessons that I have learned and that have helped me

> *"Change is hard at first, messy in the middle and gorgeous at the end."*
>
> Author Unknown

through the years. These lessons have also helped me just to get through. I hope that those of you who are new to home teaching as well as those choosing to continue to home teach can apply some of what I've discovered.

1. Discover Your Child's Learning Style.

It is important to learn your child's learning style. There are four general learning styles, and your child could fit into one of these categories or a combination of them.

These learning styles are visual, auditory, reading/writing, and kinesthetic.

Visual learners learn best when the information is seen. They process information through images rather than words so use pictures, graphs, charts, maps, and flowcharts to teach concepts and ideas.

Auditory learners, as you may have figured out by now, process information better through the spoken word. They process information through speeches, lectures, and discussions. So if you discover this about your child, keep talking and have your child talk back to you. Also, use audiobooks and other hearing aids to help your child understand and retain information.

Reading/writing learners love the written word. Give your reading/writing learner plenty of reading and writing assignments. Use books and novels and have them write book reports and take lots of notes.

Finally, kinesthetic learners process information through physical activities. In other words, they need to move and touch. Kinesthetic learners love practicing concepts so make your teaching physical through experiments, exercises, and simulations. Many kinesthetic students are labeled as hyper and not able to stay still. They may tap their feet, roll their pencil, and sway. In reality,

I have come to find that my son learns better when he is moving, bouncing a ball, rolling a pencil between his fingers, etc.

Use this time to discover how your child learns as this may change the course of your child's education because you will discover how your child understands and retains information. There are different learning style questionnaires on the Internet to help you with this or you may need to observe or find out through trial and error. Research curricula and programs catered to these learning styles. There are plenty available online. Knowledge is power and by knowing your child's unique learning style you can customize their education which, in turn, will benefit them for years to come.

2. Use Your Child's Interests as a Way to Improve their Skills.
Have your children research a topic they know nothing about and write about what they have learned. This gives your child the opportunity to take the lead in their own education and allows them to be the teacher and you the student. This type of activity accomplishes several objectives:

 a. It will increase their interest in research.
 b. It teaches your child to use the Internet to seek out and gather information, not just for game play or to watch videos.
 c. It will dramatically improve their writing skills. Your child will want to write about the new discovery, and if their writing skills aren't the best, you can take the time to constructively correct their writing and show them ways

to improve so that the research that they initiated will sound its best.

d. It will encourage your non-writer to write. My youngest son, Thomas, hates to write. However, since starting this activity, he looks forward to it because he always writes about his favorite subject, geography.

e. Whatever topic your child chooses, you could count it as a subject or a combination of subjects.

My son, Stephen, researched and discovered that there are different layers of the Internet: the web, the deep web, and the dark web and that the majority of the Internet is the deep web. Before then, he didn't know that and, frankly, neither did I. The best part of home learning is not just the joy and the excitement I feel when my sons discover something new or finally grasp a concept that we spent days, if not weeks, trying to understand, but when my sons teach ME something. Since we began this weekly activity, I have learned a lot. I learned about the religion of Jediism, that China is the world's number one producer of bananas, that people's feet have been appearing for years on the shores of Canada (Yes, I said "feet"), and that the Nile River is the combination of the White Nile River and the Blue Nile River, just to name a few.

3. Develop a Routine. Have a schedule, but don't make it rigid. I understand that some children need structure. In fact, some of you need structure. However, I believe that consistency is the key to success, not rigidity. As homeschoolers, you can determine what your day will be. Start off with a schedule and adjust as needed. For example, you may want to start your school day at 9am or start it at noon. Some days I've started learning time at 3pm. Then decide your subject order. Maybe start with science, then math, then reading, etc., and continue that order but the time can be flexible. Ask them what they would like to learn first. By starting with their favorite subject it starts the day with great anticipation. Then, alternate with a subject that's their least favorite. If your child is old enough, involve them in the making of their schedule. Always, keep in mind that you control your routine, make changes as needed, and have fun.

4. Use Board Games, Logic Games, and Puzzles. Use puzzles and board games to teach or improve skills. It might sound elementary, but there are so many types of puzzles for every subject.

They improve critical thinking and logic skills. For example, I used GeoPuzzles to teach my sons geography. I use Monopoly and CashFlow to teach real estate and investing, Scrabble to improve spelling and vocabulary, Sudoku and Clue to teach logic skills. Games are a great way to improve and teach because your child is learning by doing and they're having fun doing it.

5. Teach Short. Break Short. Teach for 30 to 45 minutes and then have a 15 to 20 minute break. It will do wonders for you and your child. If your child is kinesthetic, make it even (for example, 20 minutes of teaching followed by a 20 minute break). I believe our brains are like sponges. You know that a sponge absorbs only so much water and then the excess will not absorb. I have found that my children can only absorb so much information and anything over the limit will not "sink" in. So teach short and break short.

6. Create a Tag Team. Sometimes, I need help and you will, too. During my teaching time, my sons ask amazing, out of this world questions and I don't have a clue about the answers. That's when I make the "tag" (a wrestling reference—I was a huge wrestling fan back in the day). My tag team partners are YouTube, Google Search, Google Maps, Google Earth, and other online resources. Some home learning parents shy away from technology, but I embrace it to a point. If it is a video, always watch it with your child and watch several videos so that you get different perspectives. Look at images, also.

7. Do the Switch. You don't always have to stick to the script. Your child may have a question that may or may not have anything to do with what you're teaching. Do the switch and answer their question. First, relax because it may have disrupted your planned time then do the switch. Switch the conversation. If you know the answer, provide it. If you don't, research it and discover something new at the same time as your child. Are you getting a central theme? If the video or the image or the information spawns more questions from your child, do more research until they're satisfied. If your child's curiosity takes over, let it! Sometimes your teaching period is just answering your child's questions and that's it. You can finish what you were going to teach your child the next time.

8. Use Life as Your Textbook. One of the joys of my home teaching is having daily conversations with my sons about life and the things going on around them. Use your life lessons and current events. Subscribe to your local newspaper. You can use the news for every kind of subject. Use a topic (age appropriate, of course) from each section of the newspaper as follows:

- ◊ The Whole Newspaper—English and Grammar (point out the types of sentences, paragraph structure, the use of active vs. passive voice)
- ◊ Front Page—US Geography, US History, Any Subject
- ◊ World News—World Geography, International Affairs, World History
- ◊ Metro—Local geography, Civics, Criminal Justice
- ◊ Business—Finance, Accounting, Math, Investing
- ◊ Sports–Physical Education, Math (points, standings and averages)
- ◊ Home & Garden—Life Science, Art
- ◊ Weather—Earth Science, Physical Science, Geography
- ◊ Obituaries—Biography
- ◊ Comics—Art, English
- ◊ Food–Cooking, Nutrition, Math

9. Don't Force It. Skip It. If your child doesn't understand a new concept right away, skip it, move on to something else, and return to that concept in a couple of days. Although you may have skipped it, the brain is still working. You planted the seed of the concept. While your child is trying to understand the new concept, review concepts that they have mastered in order to remind them that the mastered concepts were also new at one time.

You may need to research a different way of explaining the concept. You may need to have someone else explain what you are trying to teach (e.g., a YouTube video, another adult, another child, a tutor). Don't worry, the light bulb will shine. It may take days. It may take weeks. It will happen. Continue to move forward.

It took my son a long time to comprehend the basic principles of Algebra. Yes, he was discouraged and so was I, especially since I LOVE Algebra. I started with Life of Fred, then I moved to Khan Academy lessons, then I tried different YouTube videos; nothing seemed to work. He wasn't getting it. The doubting thoughts came: "I can't do this. This isn't going to work out. He needs a tutor." Then, the dreaded questions came from him: "Why do I need to learn this? What am I going to use it for? " So I had to take a deep breath. I had to be creative. Then I remembered that he doesn't like math, but he likes finance. I researched videos and articles that used financial scenarios and equations that explained the same algebraic concepts that he couldn't understand. It was a success. He's still not a fan, but we advanced. Yes, it took a long time, but home teaching gives you that flexibility to take as long as you need for your child to master a concept. The blessing is that once your child gets it, they got it.

NOTES/THINGS TO REMEMBER

Chapter 10
THE METHODS

I know there are many images of children sitting around a table with piles of books around, but did you know that there are different methods or approaches to home teaching? Research each one to determine which method is right for you, your child, your family, and your schedule.

> *"They laugh at me because I'm different; I laugh at them because they're all the same."*
>
> *Unknown*

The School-At-Home Method. School-At-Home method is the most common method for many new home teachers who remove their children from the local school system. It is also called traditional homeschooling. It includes using a "boxed curriculum," which is a full curriculum of textbooks, laid-out schedules, quizzes and tests, and grading sheets for every subject. This method works best for families who wish to maintain a strict schedule with formal, planned lesson plans and activities, and most importantly, you decide on the curriculum.

The School-At-Home method can get rather expensive. If you choose this method, you can go to used book stores, online selling sites like eBay, and used curriculum fairs because families who use textbooks usually do not allow their children to write in them in hopes of reselling the curriculum after use.

The Classical Method. The classical method focuses on the idea of teaching students the art of learning in four stages: preparation, grammar, dialectic, and rhetoric. The preparation stage focuses on reading, writing, and arithmetic. The grammar stage engages the student in collections and composition. The dialectic stage encompasses study and research. The final stage, rhetoric, focuses on communicating the information that has been gathered in the previous stages. Through these methods, students are able to reason, record, relate, and communicate in any subject.

The Charlotte Mason Approach. Charlotte Mason was an 18th century English educator and the Charlotte Mason method teaches concepts through real-life situations and incorporates a lot of literature to help instill a love for it. The Charlotte Mason approach uses methods including copy work, which is the writing of a narrative verbatim to practice handwriting, spelling, and grammar; narration, the process of having your child telling back something that they have seen or heard; and living books, using books written by author passionate about a subject instead of textbooks. This method tests students on what they know through discussion rather than traditional tests. Families using this method can purchase curricula or develop their own program and apply the Charlotte Mason method.

The Montessori Method. This method was named after the Italian educator and medical doctor, Maria Montessori, who primarily focused on how young children learn. With the Montessori method, the child directs the learning while the parent guides the child's education by customizing curricula and activities with their child's interests. It discourages television and technology while encouraging nature and the outdoors. The Montessori method allows your child to discover and learn at their own pace.

The Waldorf Approach. The Waldorf approach, also known as the Steiner Educational Philosophy, was created by Rudolf Steiner in the early 1900s. The Waldorf approach focuses on learning through activities, play, the arts, and nature. Families looking for low-cost home education might consider the Waldorf approach because no standard textbooks are used during the early elementary years. It encourages your child to create their own books through research, exploration, and discovery. For higher grade levels, the Waldorf approach recommends teaching subjects or topics in 3-6 periods or 'blocks" of in-depth study for each subject. This keeps children focused on one subject at a time instead of teaching multiple subjects in a day.

The Unit Studies Method. The Unit Studies Method is another low cost method for homeschoolers. It allows students to study subjects or topics in more detail for weeks at a time so that students are able to explore and master the topics. It incorporates a range of activities to make the studies interesting, and students were able to retain more information.

The Unschooling Method. The Unschooling Method is student-led learning focusing on the interests of the child by using everyday experiences without using formal lessons. Your unschooled child picks what they want to learn and creates their own education path, similarly to self-directed courses in college. Unschooling allows children to learn through curiosity and their natural instincts as children learn to walk and talk. Parents may direct their child's interests by stimulating their interests in a certain field of study.

The Eclectic Method. The Eclectic Method is usually the end result of trying a variety of the preceding homeschooling approaches. When you combine the educational goals you have for your children with your observation of their specific interests, strengths, and weaknesses, you are able to mix and match the programs and tools that will fulfill both. You may become eclectic as your child grows and as you come to recognize your child's strengths, weaknesses, abilities, and interests, as well as when your schedule changes due to life changes, and you become more aware of which methods work and which do not.

Methods may also coincidence with curricula. Since homeschooling is inherently flexible, the curriculum, if you choose to use a curriculum, should depend on your method and your style. Please understand that you, as the parent, should decide the best curricula, if any, for your child. If they are older children, you can include them in the decision as well.

There are plenty of books and websites dedicated to each method so you can do your research to determine what might be best for your child. I've used all of these methods at one time or another during the last 11 years. Now, I'm using the eclectic method by combining classical, traditional, and Charlotte Mason, depending on the subject. I used each of the methods to accomplish a goal for a particular season. I changed my method when I felt that it wasn't accomplishing my goal, meaning my sons weren't engaged, they were frustrated, or they were bored. Home teaching allows you to be flexible. Try different methods. See what works. If you find one that works, stick with it. If it doesn't, move on. Remember to base your teaching on what is the most effective at the appropriate time.

NOTES/THINGS TO REMEMBER

Chapter 11
USEFUL RESOURCES

There are a lot of great resources to assist home teachers in their journey. I want to share a few resources that helped me along the way.

CursiveLogic (cursivelogic.com) is a great cursive mastery program that teaches lowercase letters by their four distinctive shapes rather than teaching the letters in alphabetical order. Uppercase letters are taught after mastering the lowercase letters.

College Prep Genius (www.collegeprepgenius.com) provides test-taking strategies for college entrance exams and other standardized tests as well as scholarship tips and resources.

Easy Peasy (www.allinonehomeschool.com) is a Christian online homeschooling curriculum from K-12.

Ebay (www.ebay.com) has been a great resource for most of my home teaching supplies. Many homeschoolers sell their used curricula and supplies on Ebay so you can find great deals.

> *"It's good to be blessed. It's better to be a blessing."*
> *Author Unknown*

Homeschool Buyers Co-op (www.homeschoolbuyersco-op.com) is a resource for affordable homeschool curricula and supplies.

Homeschool Legal Defense Association (www.hslda.org) helps protect the rights of homeschooling families, helps you understand the laws of your state, and provides legal representation, when necessary.

Life of Fred Math (lifeoffred.uniquemath.com) is a full, unconventional math curriculum from elementary to college that follows the life story of a 5-year-old math professor. If you have a child that loves math or hates math, but enjoys a great story, Life of Fred Math might work for you. I would suggest that you do not allow your child to write in these books. Life of Fred books are always in high demand and you can resell them when you're finished.

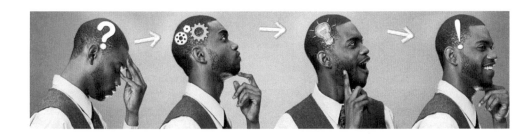

Pizza Hut Book It! Program (www.bookitprogram.com) is a program that encourages K-6 students to achieve reading goals set by their teacher. Students are rewarded with stickers and certificates for free pizza. The program runs every year from October to March.

NOTES/THINGS TO REMEMBER

Chapter 12
HELPFUL WEBSITES AND APPS

There are many educational websites and apps that are available these days to help you and your child. I have boys so I used game-based learning as a tool for teaching for many years and still do. Not all of the following websites and apps are game-

> *"I have never let my schooling interfere with my education."*
> *Mark Twain*

based, but I've used each one at one time or another to help me accomplish my teaching goals. To be honest, I've tried many websites and I could list a lot more but these are the ones that left a lasting impression on my sons.

BrainPop (brainpop.com) is an animated app of educational videos for students for Science, Social Studies, English, Math, Arts & Music, Health, and Technology. BrainPop offers free videos as well as a free daily lesson. You will need to pay a fee to view and use all of its content.

DragonBox Algebra (dragonbox.com) is a game-based app that teaches the basic applications of algebra in a fun way. DragonBox Algebra 5+ is for children ages 5 to 11. DragonBox Algebra 12+ is fun but covers more advanced topics in mathematics and algebra for children ages 12 and older as well as adults.

Duolingo (duolingo.com) is a foreign language website and app with more than 30 languages available with lessons. It is a free with a premium service available for a fee.

Elevate (elevateapp.com) is a brain training app but it is also a great teaching tool for Math, English Grammar, Reading Comprehension, and more. I would suggest this for middle and high schoolers, but don't let that stop you if you wish to use it for your young ones. There is a fee for using Elevate.

iCivics (icivics.org) is a website and app that has free lesson plans, curricula, and games to teach civics education. It was founded by retired Supreme Court Justice Sandra Day O'Connor.

Kahoot (kahoot.com) is a website with a vast collection of learning content of videos and games. I began using it for my game-based teaching, but Kahoot has expanded to include videos and self-study features. You can use its pre-prepared tests or you can make your own.

Khan Academy (khanacademy.org) is an expert-created content and resource for every subject and grade. It consists of video instruction followed by quizzes and tests. Khan Academy is always free.

Outschool.com (outschool.com) is an online school with over 8000 video chat classes for K-Science, Art, English, Social Studies, Life Skills, and more! Choose from one-time class to semester long classes. There is tuition depending on the class.

Typing.com (typing.com) is a website to teach typing and computer learning skills for beginners as well as improves typing skills for non-beginners. It is a free with a premium service available for a fee.

Understood.org (understood.org) is a resource website for supporting students who think and learn differently.

NOTES/THINGS TO REMEMBER

_____

_____

_____

_____

_____

_____

_____

_____

_____

_____

_____

_____

_____

_____

Chapter 13
WORDS DEFINED

Distance Learning—when a teacher and a student are physically separate from each other during instruction. This includes online education. This is not homeschooling. However, distance learning can be a tool in homeschooling.

Dual Enrollment—when your homeschooler enrolls in online college courses or courses at another educational institution like a community college in addition to their work at home.

> *"A person finds joy in giving an apt reply—and how good is a timely word!"*
> Proverbs
> 15:23
> (NIV)

Co-op—an abbreviation for homeschool cooperative. A co-op is a program where homeschool families attend classes and programs, gather for field trips, and socialize. Co-ops usually meet at least once per week.

Curriculum—a list of subjects or courses that you decide for your child's education.

Copywork—written passages that are carefully copied verbatim including copying the punctuation and style. Copywork is used to help children appreciate the written word as well as learn to read, write, and spell. You can use the Bible, any type of literature, even speeches such as Martin Luther King's "I Have A Dream" speech.

Homeschooling/Home Education—education of children outside of the public or private school system.

Homeschool Portfolio—an accumulation of teaching and learning materials that provide evidence of what your child has learned and their progress. Your portfolio may include but is not limited to syllabi, lists of materials used (text and resource books, online learning transcripts, computer programs), assignment samples from each subject, reading logs, participation and awards certificates, field trip pictures, writing samples, and anything that will best represent your homeschool activities. Portfolios can be electronic with scanned documents and uploaded pictures or hard paper copies organized in accordion folders, color-coded files, or three-ring binders, or by note booking.

Homeschool Portfolio Review—an evaluation of your homeschool activities and materials for *your* current school year. The type of portfolio review varies from state to state, and can occur annually, bi-annual, or quarterly. Portfolio reviews are to show your child's progress through the year, and are not meant to be an indictment on what you teach or how you teach. You may choose to have your portfolio reviewed by a homeschool representative of your local public school system, or an oversight coordinator if you are a member of an umbrella program.

Homeschool Days—reserved hours or days at museums, recreation centers, and other institutions when specially-designed programs are offered to provide hands-on learning experiences for homeschool families.

Manipulatives—a term used to describe objects that are manipulated by learners in order to create a hands-on learning experience and make concepts easier to understand. The term is most often used in mathematics, but manipulatives are also available for other subjects, such as reading and science.

Notebooking—a method used to creatively journalize or track homeschool studies and learning experiences by recording them on pages in notebooks or 3-ring binders. Homeschoolers who notebook record notes or write thoughts about what they are studying. They may use images, drawings, and other visual aids to help display their findings.

Oversight—another name for an umbrella program. Oversight programs will help you meet your state board education requirements, and review your portfolio and report the information to the state board. In lieu of meeting with a representative of your county board of education, you will be reviewed by your oversight program.

Student Educational Plan (SEP)—a written plan designed to plan your child's education and meet a child's learning needs and can be developed for your child to receive special education. The SEP is similar to the Individualized Evaluation Plan (IEP) in the traditional school system.

Umbrella—An umbrella school is an alternative education school that oversees the homeschooling of children to fulfill government requirements. Some umbrella schools provide a complete curriculum, some make suggestions, and some allow parents complete control over curriculum choices. Students in this arrangement are considered to be enrolled in the umbrella school even though they are educated at home.

NOTES/THINGS TO REMEMBER

_____

_____

_____

_____

_____

_____

_____

_____

_____

_____

_____

_____

_____

_____

TRIALS AND SUCCESSES: EFFECTIVE TEACHING AND LEARNING AT HOME

Chapter 14
SUMMARIES AND THOUGHTS

The quote from Maya Angelou is so true and something that we should remember while home teaching. Yes, I do get frustrated when I feel as if we're going one step forward and ten steps back. Then, I have to remember to be the encourager because the last thing I need is for my child to get discouraged and feel like they are a failure. Step out of the room. Take a breather. You don't want to say something that you will regret later. Children have long memories, especially about how you made them feel. Here are some other points to remember:

> "I've learned that people will forget what you said, people will forget what you did, but people will never forget how you made them feel."
> *Maya Angelou*

Accept Them for Who They Are and Use Their Interests to Teach. Each child learns differently and at different paces, even in families. The child's interest plays a huge part in how they learn a topic. Meet your child where they are and guide them along. The pace may be fast as a rabbit or as slow as a snail. For example, Thomas can tell you where Egypt is located, its latitude, the countries it borders, and its capital. Stephen does not remember a lot about Egypt's geographical features, but he can tell you about its history. Why? Thomas loves geography and Stephen loves history. So when I want Thomas to learn about a topic, I always include something about geography to get the momentum going. With Stephen, I begin with history. Then I proceed to incorporate what they would consider

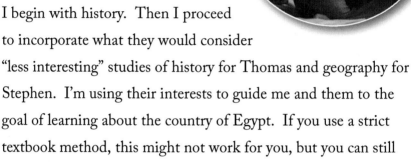

"less interesting" studies of history for Thomas and geography for Stephen. I'm using their interests to guide me and them to the goal of learning about the country of Egypt. If you use a strict textbook method, this might not work for you, but you can still apply it to extracurricular activities and life skills.

Sculpt Your Child's Education to Them and Them Alone.
Please understand that you do not need to measure your homeschooled child according to any measurement established by a school official or anybody else. Homeschooling not only tailors your child's education to their needs, their abilities, and their gifts, but it focuses on mastery. When your child learns a concept and can demonstrate that skill one day, one week, and one month afterwards, they have mastered that skill and therefore they have learned it. Teaching for a test is not learning. Teaching to master is.

Work on Both Strengths and Areas of Growth. Homeschooling allows us to know our child's strengths as well as areas of growth and work on both. Many times we focus on the areas of growth and leave their strengths alone. You may not have to spend as much time on your child's strengths but it is important to keep them strong.

Regarding areas of growth, I choose that term instead of saying "weaknesses" because "weaknesses" has a negative connotation. "Areas of growth" gives your child the perception that they can grow and improve in any subject or topic, even if it takes a little longer than usual. They will strive to get better with your encouragement and their dedication. These successes build confidence and their area of growth might indeed become a strength.

Help Your Child Identify Their Gifts and Interests. We need to help our children identify their unique gifts, keep alive their inner drive to learn and grow in their gifts. When students discover knowledge for themselves, it will last a lifetime. Through the development of genuine self-esteem, children pursue interests that delight and intrigue them, and lead them to the path and fulfill the purpose for their lives.

Break Down Your Mountain. If your child is having a tough time understanding a concept, break it into smaller lessons spreading them over several days. Break down your "mountain" so that you can conquer one small "hill" at a time, and count each mastered assignment as a victory. These small victories, no matter the age of your child, will build their confidence. It will also increase your confidence as well as reduce your blood pressure.

Listen To Your Child. I ask my sons about our homeschool. I want their opinion on the programs they use, the online classes in which I enroll them, or if they liked the co-op that we chose for the year. We make adjustments if something's not working. I think this is the key to homeschooling, particularly the upper grades. Being part of the decision process makes them more engaged and proactive in their studies and ultimately, they're becoming true independent learners, using skills that will last a lifetime. It's amazing how often they come to me now and want to share with me something they researched.

Take a Break From Traditional Methods. You can break from traditional schooling out of textbooks and worksheets by performing activities that cover a range of subjects at the same time. For example, I love cooking with my boys. Do you know that cooking can cover a wide range of subjects?

Here's a breakdown of what you can cover with a 60-minute cooking lesson (including preparation):

◊ Math—calculating measurements and conversions
◊ Reading—reading recipes
◊ Writing—writing a shopping list
◊ Science—explaining how heat energy irreparably changes the properties of foods, boiling point, stages of matter
◊ Nutrition—self-explanatory
◊ Art—creatively presenting the food, describing the different food colors
◊ Life Skills—learning how to cook

Look for activities that won't take all day to do. Look at the cooking example; you can cover seven subjects in 60 minutes. You can then take the rest of the day to explore, discover, pursue their interests, review, redo, or master. Use your time to be out-of-the box. Your child will appreciate it.

Appreciate The Student-To-Teacher Ratio. I understand some student-to-teacher ratios in traditional schools can be as high as 30:1. At home, the ratio is very low. The low student-to-teacher ratio is an advantage for your child because the time is spent teaching, discovering, and learning and is used solely for the benefit of your child. This is true whether you teach yourself, use online classes, attend co-op classes, or have student-led learning.

Use Your Teaching Time as a Time of Discovery for Your Child and for You. Give your child the opportunity to discover what they like and what they don't like. My husband often tells me, "It's not either/or, it's both/and." Home teaching/learning emphasizes the flexibility to use the time to teach AND a time to discover. They will eventually discover their niche and their gift. You may know before they do. They may know before you do.

Encourage Reading By Using the Pizza Hut Book-It! Program. If you have a child who is 11 years or younger (K-6) and you have a Pizza Hut near you, I would encourage you to enroll in the Pizza Hut Book-It! Program. Although the Book-It! Program caters to traditional schools, you can register as a homeschooler. You set a monthly reading goal based on their level and ability and if they meet the goal, your child will receive stickers and a free one-topping personal pizza. My sons looked forward to getting their free pizza so this program worked out marvelously for us and for years, we stayed in the library because of it.

Use Your Local Library. When my sons were younger, we were at the library almost every day, in part because we were enrolled in the Pizza Hut Book-It program. But in addition to the obvious benefits of checking out books for free, the library had many great programs from book readings to science exhibitions to Lego classes to chess clubs.

Your library is another tag partner in providing education for your child. More importantly, most library programs are free. Check out the upcoming events calendar and plan ahead.

Encourage Your Child Through the Struggle. If your child struggles with the "core" subjects like math or reading, it's not the end of the world. Work with them. Take small steps. Don't pressure, encourage. Build up those small victories. Give them the time to grow. I am a witness to how beneficial this approach is. You know, we want our children to be prodigies, but we all are not blessed with prodigies. Just the same, we want wealth. Some are born with wealth. Some will have to work for it. It's okay to work for it. The appreciation will be greater.

Use Copywork and Teach Cursive. You can use copywork to accomplish so many different tasks. You can use it for word recognition, grammar and syntax, spelling, reading comprehension, memorization, and discussion. It's a great way for your child to learn so many ways at one time. I also used copy work to help strengthen my son's handwriting and their cursive. Yes, I taught them cursive. It is a lost art, but I think it is very important to know. You want your children to be able to sign their name and to be versatile.

Teach History. Right now, the world is focused on STEM and STEAM education since some much of the world is going digital. STEM stands for Science, Technology, Engineering, and Math. STEAM is Science, Technology, Engineering, Art, and Math. But children need to know history. Nothing is new under the sun and history gives perspective on current events, and why things are the way they are. Why do certain countries in the Middle East despise countries like the United States and the United Kingdom? Why is racism so prominent in the American "Bible Belt"? Why do Brazilians speak Portuguese instead of Spanish?

The standard American curriculum focuses on American and European history, and Christian curriculums focus on Jewish history. But children, no matter what race, need to know ALL history, the good, the bad, and the ugly. Of course, teach what is appropriate for their age, but teach it. Don't rely on the typical textbooks. Visit museums. View documentaries. Go deeper and get enlightened.

You Are Not Alone. You are not alone because there are thousands of home teaching parents that are experiencing many of the feelings, doubts, and the range of emotions just like you do or you will. If you feel overwhelmed, contact a fellow homeschool parent or homeschool support group.

NOTES/THINGS TO REMEMBER

Chapter 15

THE FINAL WORD

> *And we know that all things work together for good to those who love God, to those who are the called according to His purpose.*
>
> *Romans 8:28 (NKJV)*

Now, you may not believe any of the preceding information. You may be a proponent of formal education. You may believe that homeschoolers are undereducated. That's fine. I respect that. This book was not written for you as I mentioned in the first paragraph. This book detailed my calling to homeschool and how I witnessed the incredible metamorphosis of my sons, from not being able to hold a pencil to writing and typing multi-page essays, from counting with their fingers to solving linear equations, and everything in between.

My final analogy summarizes my overall thoughts of home education. Early in our homeschooling years, Stephen and I planted four beans in four Styrofoam cups to illustrate how plants grow from a bean, a typical lesson in early education. A week later, we started to see the sprouts from three of the four plants. Stephen was extremely excited. However, we were wondering if something had happened to the fourth bean. It wasn't growing.

I was about to throw it away, but I decided to wait to see what it would do. We continued watering the plant. We kept it in the sun. We talked to it. Looking back, I now realized that we were giving the fourth bean extra love and care while continuing to care for the other three plants. Soon, we saw a little sprout. It wasn't growing as fast as the other three, but it was growing. The first three plants began to grow small leaves while the fourth plant still had a little sprout. The first plants grew taller and taller at the same pace and the fourth plant was still very much behind. Stephen was amazed, and frankly, so was I.

Two weeks later, the three plants had grown tall and were showing nice, thick, green leaves, but their growth slowed. However, the fourth plant's growth accelerated. Then, something incredible happened. The three plants stopped growing altogether while the fourth plant grew taller and taller. That fourth plant, the one that we almost gave up on, the one I almost threw away, the one that took its time growing, the one that was always behind the others, eventually bypassed the other three and grew to be the tallest plant with the fullest, greenest, healthiest leaves.

This story reminds me and, hopefully, you, that our children are unique and they all might start out the same way as babies, but they don't grow the same way, learn the same way, and learn at the same pace. We should never judge the pace of a learning child because we have no idea what lies ahead if we continue to nurture them and let them grow. That is what home education is all about. It was a daring choice that my husband and I made 11 years ago and we would make the same choice over and over again. I wish you well on your journey as I continue on mine as we educate our children to leave a lasting legacy for generations to come.

"Whenever you find yourself doubting how far you can go, just remember how far you have come. Remember everything you have faced, all the battles you have won, and all the fears you have overcome."

Author Unknown

About the Author

Stephanie Carter is passionate about homeschooling. Her passion grows out of a deep desire to see children, particularly African-American boys, fulfill their life's purpose through an education customized to the child's interests and gifts using an out-of-the-box, eclectic approach. She feels that is it important for parents to know about educational freedom and to empower parents to take complete educational responsibility and place their child's education into their hands. Stephanie is the wife of award-winning Gospel Artist and entrepreneur Phillip Carter and homeschooling mother of two wonderful sons, Stephen and Thomas.

Made in the USA
Middletown, DE
20 August 2020

16169792R00062